# Graduates
## *Are Special*

COMPILED BY
## LUCY MEAD

GRAMERCY BOOKS
NEW YORK

This 2005 edition is published by Gramercy Books, an imprint of Random House Value Publishing, a division of Random House, Inc., New York.

Gramercy is a registered trademark and the colophon is a trademark of Random House, Inc.

Random House
New York • Toronto • London • Sydney • Auckland
www.randomhouse.com

Interior design: Karen Ocker Design, New York

Printed and bound in Singapore

A catalog record for this title is available from the Library of Congress.

ISBN 0-517-22481-X

10 9 8 7 6 5 4 3 2 1

# Graduates
## *Are Special*

"Would you tell me please, which way I ought to go from here?"
"That depends a good deal on where you want to get to," said the Cat."
"I don't much care where—" said Alice.
"Then it doesn't matter which way you go;" said the Cat.
"—so long as I get somewhere," Alice added as an explanation.
"Oh, you're sure to do that," said the Cat, "if you only walk long enough."

LEWIS CARROLL, *Alice in Wonderland*

Education is an admirable thing, but it is well to remember from time to time that nothing worth knowing can be taught.

OSCAR WILDE

Now what I want is, Facts. Teach these boys and girls nothing but Facts. Facts alone are wanted in life. Plant nothing else, and root out everything else . . . Stick to Facts, sir!

CHARLES DICKENS, *Hard Times*

It's not whether you get knocked down, it's whether you get up.

VINCE LOMBARDI

How have I profited from all my years of education? I know
most of the answers to *Jeopardy*.

REGINA, AGE 86

When your dreams turn to dust, vacuum.

DESMOND TUTU

Believe you can and you're halfway there.

THEODORE ROOSEVELT

One of the great things about books is sometimes
there are some fantastic pictures.

GEORGE W. BUSH in *U.S. News*

If you want to succeed you should strike out on new paths rather
than travel the worn paths of accepted success.

JOHN D. ROCKEFELLER

Never let the fear of striking out get in your way.

BABE RUTH

How far you go in life depends on your being tender with
the young, compassionate with the aged, sympathetic with
the striving, and tolerant of the weak and the strong—because
someday you will have been all of these.

GEORGE WASHINGTON CARVER

The true measure of a man is how he treats someone
who can do him absolutely no good.

ANN LANDERS

Approach life like a voyage on a schooner. Enjoy the view. Explore
the vessel. Make friends with the captain. Fish a little. And then
get off when you get home.

MAX LUCADO

Education is not the filling of a pail, but the lighting of a fire.

WILLIAM BUTLER YEATS

Anyone who stops is old, whether at 20 or 80. Anyone who keeps
learning stays young. The greatest thing in life is to keep your
mind young.

HENRY FORD

It's easy to make a buck. It's a lot tougher to make a difference.

TOM BROKAW

Sometimes I worry about being
a success in a mediocre world.

LILY TOMLIN

If you think you are leading and turn around to see no one
following, then you are just taking a walk.

BENJAMIN HOOKS, retired Director of the NAACP

Mediocrity knows nothing higher than itself,
but talent instantly recognizes genius.

SIR ARTHUR CONAN DOYLE

Wisdom is the principal thing; therefore get
wisdom: and with all thy getting get understanding.

PROVERBS 4:7

The pupil who is never required to
do what he cannot do, never does what he can do.

JOHN STUART MILL

Do you know the difference between education and
experience? Education is when you read the fine print;
experience is what you get when you don't.

PETE SEEGER

Be wiser than other people if you
can; but do not tell them so.

LORD CHESTERFIELD

Computers are useless.
They can only give you answers.

PABLO PICASSO

A pro is someone who can do great
work when he doesn't feel like it.

ALISTAIR COOK

The roots of education are bitter, but the fruit is sweet.

ARISTOTLE

Better be wise by the misfortunes of others than by your own.

AESOP

Life isn't a matter of milestones,
but of moments.

ROSE KENNEDY

The man who views the world the same at 50
as he did at 30 has wasted 20 years of his life.

MUHAMMED ALI

You're aware the boy failed my grade school math class, I take it? And not that many years later he's teaching college. Now I ask you: Is that the sorriest indictment of the American education system you ever heard? No aptitude at all for long division, but never mind. It's him they ask to split the atom. How he talked his way into the Nobel Prize is beyond me. But then, I suppose it's like the man says, "It's not what you know...

Elementary school teacher KARL ARBEITER
about Albert Einstein

Education is an ornament in prosperity
and a refuge in adversity.

ARISTOTLE

You got to be careful if you don't know where you're going,
because you might not get there.

YOGI BERRA

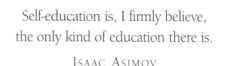

Self-education is, I firmly believe,
the only kind of education there is.

ISAAC ASIMOV

Neither birth nor sex forms a limit to genius.

CHARLOTTE BRONTE

Most of the shadows of this life are caused
by standing on one's own sunshine.

RALPH WALDO EMERSON

Experience taught me a few things. One is to listen to your gut, no
matter how good something sounds on paper.

DONALD TRUMP

The beautiful thing about learning is nobody can take it away from you.

B. B. KING

Be more concerned with your character than with your reputation. Your character is what you really are while your reputation is merely what others think you are.

DALE CARNEGIE

A professor is one who talks in someone else's sleep.

W. H. AUDEN

Homer explains that he never passed Science 101.

Marge :     "But, Homer! You're a Nuclear Technician."

Homer :    "Marge! Icksnay on the Uclearnay EchnicianTay."

Marge :     "What did you say?"

Homer :    "I don't know. I flunked Latin, too."

*The Simpsons*

Be careful what you set your heart upon,
for it will surely be yours.

JAMES BALDWIN

I am not young enough to know everything.

J. M. BARRIE, AUTHOR of *Peter Pan*

Chase after the truth like all hell and you'll free
yourself, even though you never touch its coattails.

CLARENCE DARROW

I received my best education from my mother: stay out of trouble,
always carry a clean handkerchief, and think before you speak.

SUSAN, AGE 67

The question "Who ought to be the boss?" is like asking "Who
ought to be the tenor in the quartet?" Obviously the man who can
sing tenor.

HENRY FORD

Leadership: the art of getting someone else to do something you want done because he wants to do it.

DWIGHT D. EISENHOWER

I find television very educational. Every time someone switches it on I go into another room and read a good book.

GROUCHO MARX

Thinking is more precious than all five senses.

RABBI NACHMAN OF BRATSLAV

Show me a good loser and I'll show you an idiot.

LEO DUROCHER

There's nothing so useless as doing efficiently that which should not be done at all.

PETER F. DRUCKER

Two commanders on the same field are always one too many.

GENERAL U.S. GRANT, *The Personal Memoirs of Ulysses S. Grant*

If you wou'd not be forgotten
As soon as you are dead and rotten,
Either write things worth reading,
Or do things worth the writing.

BENJAMIN FRANKLIN,
*Poor Richard's Almanack*

You gain strength, courage, and confidence by every experience in which you really stop to look fear in the face. You must do the thing which you think you cannot do.

ELEANOR ROOSEVELT

 Never mistake motion for action.

ERNEST HEMINGWAY

A big leather-bound volume makes an ideal razor strap. A thin book is useful to stick under a table with a broken caster to steady it. A large, flat atlas can be used to cover a window with a broken pane. And a thick, old-fashioned heavy book with a clasp is the finest thing in the world to throw at a noisy cat.

MARK TWAIN

Opportunities multiply as they are seized.

SUN TZU

It is better to be feared than loved, if you cannot be both.

NICCOLO MACHIAVELLI, *The Prince*

God gave men both a penis and brain, but unfortunately not enough blood supply to run both at the same time.

ROBIN WILLIAMS

I have not failed. I've just found 10,000 ways that won't work.

THOMAS ALVA EDISON

Education…has produced a vast population able to read but unable to distinguish what is worth reading.

GEORGE MACAULAY TREVELYAN, English historian

A child educated only at school is an undereducated child.

GEORGE SANTAYANA

Every exit is an entry somewhere else.

TOM STOPPARD

How many cares one loses when one decides
not to be something but to be someone.

COCO CHANEL

In the beginner's mind there are
many possibilities, but in the
expert's mind there are few.

SHUNRYU SUZUKI

Only those who dare to fail miserably can achieve greatly.

ROBERT KENNEDY

I never remember feeling tired by work, though
idleness exhausts me completely.

ARTHUR CONAN DOYLE

The difference between the impossible and the
possible lies in a person's determination.

TOMMY LASORDA

Reality is something you rise above.

LIZA MINNELLI

The only way to discover the limits of the possible is to go beyond into the impossible.

ARTHUR C. CLARKE

Whoever said money can't buy happiness didn't know where to shop.

GERTRUDE STEIN

The two most beautiful words in the
English language are "check enclosed."

DOROTHY PARKER

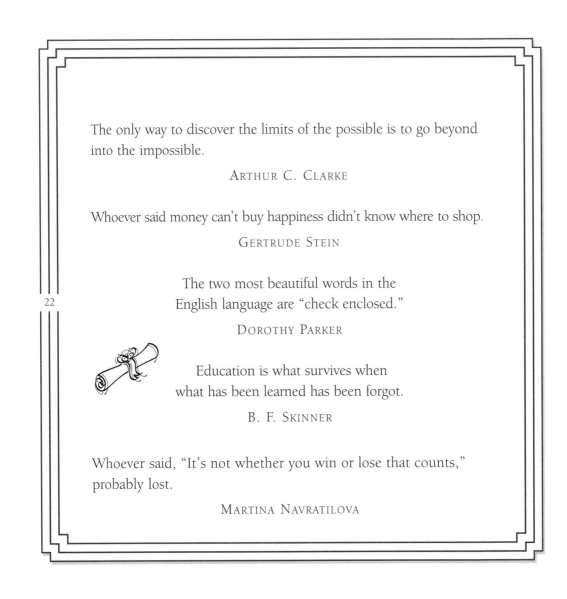

Education is what survives when
what has been learned has been forgot.

B. F. SKINNER

Whoever said, "It's not whether you win or lose that counts," probably lost.

MARTINA NAVRATILOVA

Well done is better than well said.

BENJAMIN FRANKLIN

Hold fast to dreams, for if dreams die,
life is a broken winged bird that cannot fly.

LANGSTON HUGHES

Education is a progressive
discovery of our own ignorance.

WILL DURANT

The world is filled with willing people;
some willing to work, the rest willing to let them.

ROBERT FROST

I am the world's worst salesman, therefore, I must make it easy for
people to buy.

F. W. WOOLWORTH

The artist is nothing without the gift,
but the gift is nothing without work.

EMILA ZOLA

Genius is but one percent inspiration
and ninety-nine percent perspiration.

THOMAS ALVA EDISON

When you are in any contest, you should work as if there were—to the
very last minute—a chance to lose it. This is battle. This is politics.
This is anything.

DWIGHT D. EISENHOWER

I do not feel obliged to believe that the same God who has endowed us
with sense, reason, and intellect has intended us to forego their use.

GALILEO

It's true hard work never killed anybody, but I figure, why take the chance?

RONALD REAGAN

It's kind of fun to do the impossible.

WALT DISNEY

Kites rise highest against the wind—not with it.

WINSTON CHURCHILL

The secret of success is to know something nobody else knows.

ARISTOTLE ONASSIS

One of the symptoms of an approaching nervous breakdown is the belief that one's work is terribly important.

BERTRAND RUSSELL

To be a champion, you have to believe in yourself when nobody else will.

SUGAR RAY ROBINSON

The taste of a first-rate intelligence is the ability to hold two opposed ideas at the same time, and still retain the ability to function.

F. SCOTT FITZGERALD

Rather fail with honor than succeed by fraud.

SOPHOCLES

Ferengi Rule of Acquisition: Never allow family to stand in the way of opportunity.

*Star Trek: Deep Space Nine*

Take your work seriously, but never yourself.

DAME MARGOT FONTEYN

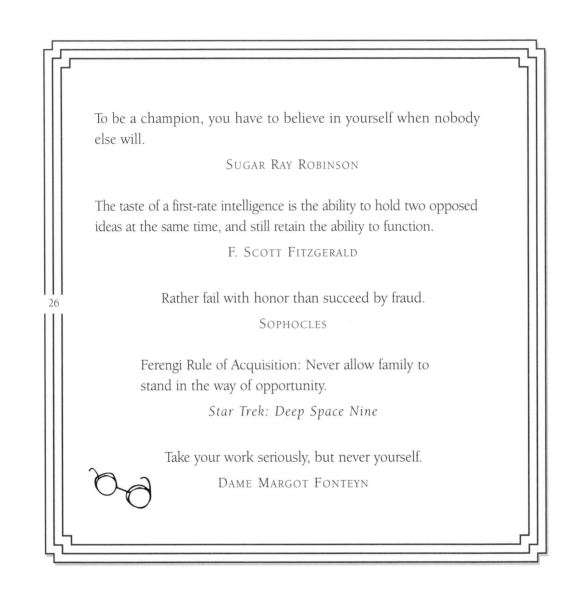

## WHAT IS SUCCESS?

To laugh often and much;
To win the respect of intelligent people and the affection
    of children;
To earn the appreciation of honest critics and endure the
    betrayal of false friends;
To appreciate beauty;
To find the best in others;
To leave the world a bit better, whether by a healthy
    child, a garden patch, or a redeemed social condition;
To know even one life has breathed easier because you
    have lived;
This is to have succeeded.

RALPH WALDO EMERSON

Never bend your head.
Always hold it high.
Look the world straight in the eye.

HELEN KELLER

You should not confuse your career with your life.

DAVIE BARRY, *Dave Barry Turns 50*

Character consists of what you
do on the third and fourth tries.

JAMES A. MICHENER

I am not afraid of storms,
I am learning how to sail my ship.

LOUISA MAY ALCOTT

Imagination is more important than knowledge.

ALBERT EINSTEIN

The greatest good you can do for another is not just to share your riches but to reveal to him his own.

BENJAMIN DISRAELI

He who hesitates is sometimes saved.

JAMES THURBER

Life is like a game of cards. The hand that is dealt you represents determinism. The way you play it is free will.

JAWAHARLAL NEHRU

See everything. Overlook a great deal. Improve a little.

POPE JOHN XXIII

Until you value yourself, you will not value your time. Until you value your time, you will not do anything with it.

M. SCOTT PECK

My grandfather told me there are two kinds of people: Those who do the work and those who take the credit. He told me to be in the first group; there was much less competition.

INDIRA GANDHI

...Character counts for a great deal more than either intellect or body in winning success in life...

THEODORE ROOSEVELT

To disagree, one doesn't have to be disagreeable.

BARRY M. GOLDWATER

People seldom improve when they have
no other model but themselves to copy after.

OLIVER GOLDSMITH

Good name and honor are worth more
all the gold and jewels ever mined.

HARRY S. TRUMAN

Do not do what you would undo if caught.

LEAH ARENDT

You grow up the day you have your first real laugh at yourself.

ETHEL BARRYMORE

Time is a dressmaker specializing in alterations.

FAITH BALDWIN

Slow and steady wins the race.

AESOP, "The Hare and the Tortoise"

Learning without thought is labor lost.

CONFUCIUS

Success has ruin'd many a Man.

BENJAMIN FRANKLIN, *Poor Richard's Almanack*

I am convinced that it is of primordial importance to learn more every year than the year before. After all, what is education but a process by which a person begins to learn how to learn.

PETER USTINOV

Graduation day is tough for adults. They get to the ceremony as parents. They come home as contemporaries. After twenty-two years of child-rearing, they are unemployed.

Erma Bombeck

Do a common thing in an uncommon way.

Booker T. Washington

I believe you are your work. Don't trade the stuff of your life, time, for nothing more than dollars. That's a rotten bargain.

Rita Mae Brown

 A strong, positive self-image is the best possible preparation for success.

Joyce Brothers

Education is a weapon whose effects depend on who holds it in his hands and at whom it is aimed.

Joseph Stalin

And who knows? Somewhere out there in this audience may even be someone who will one day follow in my footsteps, and preside over the White House as the president's spouse. I wish him well.

Barbara Bush, commencement
address at Wellesley College

Adventure is worthwhile in itself.

Amelia Earhart

Money is not the most important thing in the world. Love is. Fortunately, I love money.

Jackie Mason

Why can't somebody give us a list of things that everybody thinks and nobody says, and another list of things that everybody says and nobody thinks?

Oliver Wendell Holmes, Sr., *The Professor at
the Breakfast-Table*, 1872

You won't arrive. It is an endless search.

SHERWOOD ANDERSON

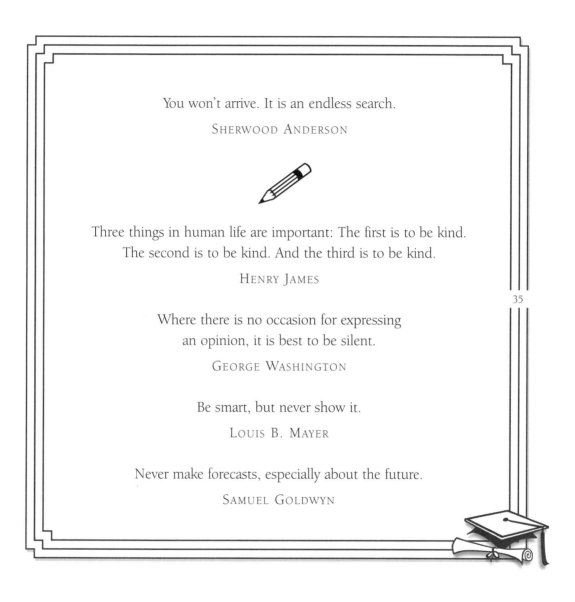

Three things in human life are important: The first is to be kind.
The second is to be kind. And the third is to be kind.

HENRY JAMES

Where there is no occasion for expressing
an opinion, it is best to be silent.

GEORGE WASHINGTON

Be smart, but never show it.

LOUIS B. MAYER

Never make forecasts, especially about the future.

SAMUEL GOLDWYN

It's important to be smart in school, but it's even more important to be smart about yourself.

IRVING BERLIN

Believe in yourself! Have faith in your abilities!

NORMAN VINCENT PEALE

Fame is a fickle food
Upon a shifting plate.

EMILY DICKINSON

Circumstances have nothing to do with success. When you have made up your mind, success is certain.

WILLIAM RANDOLPH HEARST

Success is full of promise till men get it; and then it is a last-year's nest from which the birds have flown.

HENRY WARD BEECHER, Life Thoughts, 1859

Achievement, n. The death of endeavor
and the birth of disgust.

AMBROSE BIERCE, *The Devil's Dictionary*

Associate yourself with men of good quality if you esteem
your own reputation, for 'tis better to be alone than in
bad company.

GEORGE WASHINGTON

No problem is so big and complicated
that it can't be run away from.

CHARLES M. SHULZ, *Peanuts*

The rung of a ladder was never meant to rest upon, but only to
hold a man's foot long enough to enable him to put the other
somewhat higher.

THOMAS HUXLEY, scientist and
supporter of Charles Darwin

If one cannot state a matter clearly enough so that even an intelligent twelve-year-old can understand it, one should remain within the cloistered walls of the university and laboratory until one gets a better grasp of one's subject matter.

MARGARET MEAD in *Redbook*

I think knowing what you cannot do is more important than knowing what you can.

LUCILLE BALL

The guy who invented the first wheel was an idiot. The guy who invented the other three, he was a genius.

SID CAESAR

Surround yourself with the best people you can find, delegate authority, and don't interfere.

RONALD REAGAN

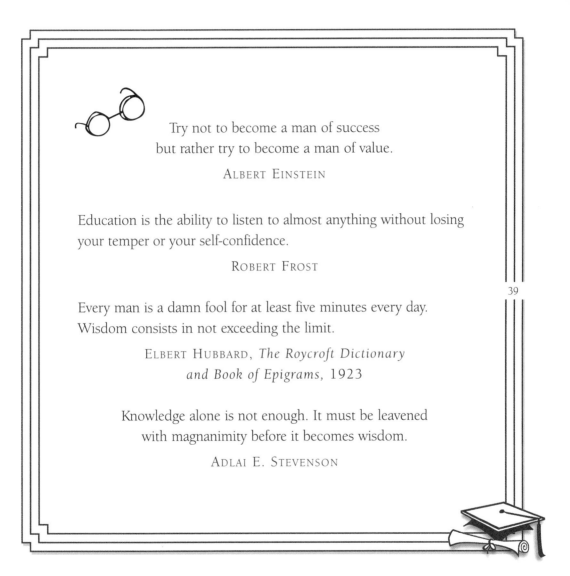

Try not to become a man of success
but rather try to become a man of value.

ALBERT EINSTEIN

Education is the ability to listen to almost anything without losing
your temper or your self-confidence.

ROBERT FROST

Every man is a damn fool for at least five minutes every day.
Wisdom consists in not exceeding the limit.

ELBERT HUBBARD, *The Roycroft Dictionary
and Book of Epigrams,* 1923

Knowledge alone is not enough. It must be leavened
with magnanimity before it becomes wisdom.

ADLAI E. STEVENSON

The quality of strength lined with tenderness is an unbeatable combination, as are intelligence and necessity when unblunted by formal education.

Maya Angelou

If you had to identify, in one word, the reason why the human race has not achieved, and never will achieve, its full potential, that word would be: "meetings."

Davie Barry, *Dave Barry Turns 50*

When dealing with people, remember you are not dealing with creatures of logic, but with creatures of emotion, creatures bristling with prejudice and motivated by pride and vanity.

Dale Carnegie

Knowledge is the treasure,<br>but judgment the treasurer of a wise man.

William Penn

Here is the test of wisdom,
Wisdom is not finally tested in schools,
Wisdom cannot be pass'd from one having it to another not
     having it,
Wisdom is of the soul, is not susceptible of proof, is its
     own proof,
Applies to all stages and objects and qualities and is content,
Is the certainty of the reality and immortality of things,
     and the excellence of things.

     WALT WHITMAN, "Song of the Open Road"

     Not in the clamor of the crowded street,
     Not in the shouts and plaudits of the throng,
     But in ourselves, are triumph and defeat.

     HENRY WADSWORTH LONGFELLOW

The trouble with being number one in the world—at anything—is that it takes a certain mentality to attain that position in the first place, and that is something of a driving, perfectionist attitude, so that once you do achieve number one, you don't relax and enjoy it.

BILLIE JEAN KING

I have learned that success is to be measured not so much by the position that one has reached in life as by the obstacles which he has overcome while trying to succeed.

BOOKER T. WASHINGTON, *Up from Slavery*

Be awfully nice to them going up,
because you're gonna meet them all coming down.

JIMMY DURANTE

All rising to a great place is by a winding stair.

ABRAHAM LINCOLN

The trouble with the rat race is
that even if you win, you're still a rat.

LILY TOMLIN

The way I see it, if you want the rainbow, you gotta
put up with the rain.

DOLLY PARTON

We are confronted with
insurmountable opportunities.

WALT KELLY, *Pogo*

He who knows enough is enough will always have enough.

LAO-TZU

The hardest years in life are those between ten and seventy.

HELEN HAYES

Perplexity is the beginning of knowledge.

KAHLIL GIBRAN, *The Prophet*

Everyone has a role in life. Sulu is the navigator. Uhura is the communications specialist. Do your own job and the ship will function more smoothly.

DAVE MARINACCIO, *All I really need to know I learned from watching Star Trek.*

A person isn't educated unless he has learned how little he already knows.

> THOMAS A FLEMING, National Teacher of the Year, 1992

Everybody who is incapable of
learning has taken to teaching.

> OSCAR WILDE

I have never let my schooling interfere with my education.

> MARK TWAIN

The word impossible is not in my dictionary. Never measure the height of a mountain, until you have reached the top. Then you will see how low it was.

> DAG HAMMARSKJOLD

Smartness runs in my family. When I went to school I was so smart my teacher was in my class for five years.

> GEORGE BURNS

## THE DRUM

daddy says the world is
a drum tight and hard
and I told him
i'm gonna beat
out my own rhythm

NIKKI GIOVANNI

If a gnat dived into your pool of knowledge,
it would break its neck.

CARY GRANT to GINGER ROGERS
in *Once Upon a Honeymoon*

I don't know a lot about anything, but I
know a little about practically everything.

VINCENT PRICE in *Laura*

Becoming number one is easier than remaining number one.

BILL BRADLEY

If a man does his best, what else is there?

GENERAL GEORGE S. PATTON

Each of us must earn our own existence. And how does anyone earn anything? Through perseverence, hard work, and desire.

SUPREME COURT JUSTICE THURGOOD MARSHALL

Victory goes to the player
who makes the next-to-last mistake.

CHESSMASTER SAVIELLY
GRIGORIEVITCH TARTAKOWER

No bird soars too high if he soars with his own wings.

WILLIAM BLAKE

Teachers open the door, but you must enter by yourself.

CHINESE PROVERB

Your mind is what makes everything else work.

KAREEM ABDUL-JABBAR

There are no secrets to success:
Don't waste time looking for them.
Success is the result of perfection,
Hard work, learning from failure,
Loyalty to those for whom you work and persistence.

GENERAL COLIN POWELL

A boss says GO while a leader says LET'S GO.

GENERAL DOUGLAS MACARTHUR

It is not the mountain we conquer but ourselves.

EDMUND HILLARY

Don't look back. Something might be gaining on you.

SATCHEL PAIGE

Even if you're on the right track,
you'll get run over if you just sit there.

WILL ROGERS

For all sad words of tongue or pen,
The saddest are these: "It might have been!"

JOHN GREENLEAF WHITTIER

Never interrupt your enemy
when he is making a mistake.

NAPOLEON BONAPARTE

When one door closes, another opens, but we often look so long and so regretfully upon the closed door that we do not see the one which has opened for us.

ALEXANDER GRAHAM BELL

A career is wonderful, but you can't
curl up with a career on a cold night.

MARILYN MONROE

Watching and listening—those are extremely important abilities to develop in yourself. Why, even when I was teaching, there were plenty of times when my students came up with better ideas than I had. And why shouldn't they. Just because I was the teacher didn't mean that I knew everything. No one can know it all.

SADIE DELANEY, *The Delaney Sisters'
Book of Everyday Wisdom*

Experience is not what happens to a man.
It is what a man does with what happens to him.

ALDOUS HUXLEY

The Golden Mean: This is an indeterminate point lying somewhere between If at first you don't succeed, try try again, and Enough is enough.

JUDITH VIORST, *Love, Guilt & The Meaning of Life, Etc.*

If at first you don't succeed, try, try again. Then quit. No use being a damn fool about it."

W. C. FIELDS

The first rule of holes: when you're in one, stop digging.

MOLLY IVINS

Always be smarter than the people who hire you.

LENA HORNE

Don't compromise yourself. You are all you've got.

JANIS JOPLIN

You may be disappointed if you fail,
but you are doomed if you don't try.

BEVERLY SILLS

Whenever I'm caught between two evils,
I take the one I haven't tried yet.

MAE WEST

If you follow all the rules, you'll never have any fun.

KATHARINE HEPBURN

You have brains in your head.
You have feet in your shoes.
You can steer yourself
any direction you choose.

You're on your own. And you know what you know.
And YOU are the guy who'll decide where to go.

DR. SEUSS, *Oh, the Places You'll Go!*

You must keep your mind on the objective, not on the obstacle.

WILLIAM RANDOLPH HEARST

Thank goodness I was never sent to school;
it would have rubbed off some of the originality.

BEATRIX POTTER

Keep your eyes on the stars,
keep your feet on the ground.

THEODORE ROOSEVELT

Education is important. After all, if you couldn't sign your name, you'd have to pay cash.

MILTON BERLE, *More of the Best of Milton Berle's Private Joke File*

As for you my fine friend,
You are a victim of disorganized thinking.
You are under the unfortunate delusion
That simply because you run away from danger,
You have no courage.
You're confusing courage with wisdom.

FRANK MORGAN, to the Cowardly Lion,
*in The Wizard of Oz*

Advice is like snow;
The softer it falls the longer it dwells upon,
And the deeper it sinks into the mind.

SAMUEL TAYLOR COLERIDGE

Only those who risk going too far
Can possibly find out how far one can go.

T.S. ELIOT

A guitar's all right, John, but you'll never earn your living by it.

JOHN LENNON'S AUNT MIMI

The greatest lesson in life is to know
that even fools are right sometimes.

WINSTON CHURCHILL

Life is like a ten-speed bike. Most of us
have gears we never use.

CHARLES SCHULZ

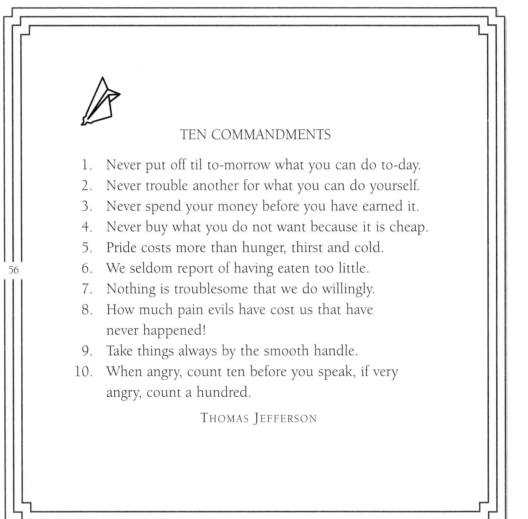

## TEN COMMANDMENTS

1. Never put off til to-morrow what you can do to-day.
2. Never trouble another for what you can do yourself.
3. Never spend your money before you have earned it.
4. Never buy what you do not want because it is cheap.
5. Pride costs more than hunger, thirst and cold.
6. We seldom report of having eaten too little.
7. Nothing is troublesome that we do willingly.
8. How much pain evils have cost us that have never happened!
9. Take things always by the smooth handle.
10. When angry, count ten before you speak, if very angry, count a hundred.

THOMAS JEFFERSON

I don't know the secret to success,
But the key to failure is to try and please everyone!

BILL COSBY

Efforts and courage are not enough
without purpose and direction.

JOHN F. KENNEDY

Do not follow where the path may lead.
Go instead where there is no path and leave a trail.

GEORGE BERNARD SHAW

There are no traffic jams along the extra mile.

ROGER STAUBACH

Life is like a dogsled team...
If you're not the lead dog, the scenery never changes

LEWIS GRIZZARD

It is more important to be of service than successful.

ROBERT KENNEDY

Education is not a cure-all, it is only a prescription, not the medicine. Hard work is still the medicine.

RON, AGE 48

The teaching is not what counts.
It is the doing that is important.

THE TALMUD

The only place where success comes before work is a dictionary.

VIDAL SASSOON

Knowing is not enough; We must apply.
Willing is not enough; We must do.

GOETHE

No! Try not. Do, or do not. There is no try.

YODA in *The Empire Strikes Back*

The reason why worry kills more people than work is
that more people worry than work.

ROBERT FROST

Obstacles don't have to stop you. If you run into a
wall, don't turn around and give up. Figure out
how to climb it, go through it, or work around it.

MICHAEL JORDAN

*All I Really Need to Know*
*I Learned in Kindergarten*

Share everything.

Play fair.

Don't hit people.

Put things back where you found them.

Clean up your own mess.

Don't take things that aren't yours.

Say you're sorry when you hurt somebody.

Wash your hands before you eat.

Flush.

Warm cookies and cold milk are good for you.

Live a balanced life—learn some and think some and draw
and paint and sing and dance and play and work every
day some.

ROBERT FULGHUM

I did not learn everything I need to know in kindergarten.

BART SIMPSON in *The Simpsons*

Your talent is God's gift to you.
What you do with it is your gift back to God.

LEO BUSCAGLIA

Experience is not what happens to a man. It is what a man does
with what happens to him.

ALDOUS HUXLEY

Seek not the things that are too hard for thee, neither search the
things that are beyond thy strength.

APOCRYPHA

Chance favors the prepared mind.

LOUIS PASTEUR

Character and personal force are the
only investments that are worth anything.

WALT WHITMAN

What's money?
A man is a success if he gets up in the morning
and goes to bed at night
and in the middle does what he wants to do.

BOB DYLAN

If you have a chance to make things better and you don't,
you're wasting your time here on earth.

ROBERTO CLEMENTE

Success has made failures of many men.

CINDY ADAMS

It is not the strongest of the species that survive, nor the most
intelligent, but the one most responsive to change

CHARLES DARWIN

Most people would succeed in small things, if they were not troubled with great ambitions.

HENRY WADSWORTH LONGFELLOW

Even if I knew that tomorrow the world would go to pieces, I would still plant my apple tree.

DR. MARTIN LUTHER KING, JR.

Winning isn't everything, it's the only thing.

VINCE LOMBARDI

You're gonna lose some ball games and you're gonna win some ball games and that's about it.

SPARKY ANDERSON

You've got to follow your passion. You've got to figure out what it is you love—who you really are. And have the courage to do that. I believe that the only courage anybody ever needs is the courage to follow your own dreams.

OPRAH WINFREY

### SHOULD YOU GO TO GRAD SCHOOL?

I am a compulsive neurotic.
I like my imagination crushed into dust.
I enjoy being a professor's slave.
My idea of a good time is using jargon and citing authorities.
I feel a deep need to continue the process of avoiding life.

MATT GROENING, *Life In Hell*

It is never too late to be what you might have been.

GEORGE ELIOT

The game isn't over till it's over.
YOGI BERRA

After all, tomorrow is another day.

MARGARET MITCHELL